COLLECTORS'
PAPERWEIGHTS

COLLECTORS' PAPERWEIGHTS

PRICE GUIDE AND CATALOGUE

PAPERWEIGHT • PRESS
SANTA CRUZ • CALIFORNIA

L.H. SELMAN LTD.

PAPERWEIGHT SPECIALISTS
761 CHESTNUT STREET
SANTA CRUZ • CALIFORNIA • 95060
TELEPHONE • 408-427-1177 • 800-538-0766

Dear Collector,

Congratulations! You have taken the first important step in learning about paperweights by ordering COLLECTORS' PAPERWEIGHTS: PRICE GUIDE AND CATALOGUE. The following pages present the finest contemporary limited editions as well as classic, museum-quality weights from the 1840s. The alphabetically listed contemporary artists, studios and companies are briefly described to you. Their individual histories, locations, philosophies and unique artistic features are outlined. Antique paperweight listings follow the contemporary entries.

This catalogue also includes a question and answer fact sheet on paperweight collecting, a selected bibliography of books and periodicals for your library, and suggested accessories to facilitate your collecting. For your benefit, we have also provided a reference list of contemporary Baccarat sulphides and Gridel animal subjects with their year of issuance. Cristal d'Albret and St. Louis sulphide subjects are also listed. Finally, a glossary has been provided to help you fully understand paperweight terminology.

Since the 1850s, paperweights have been collectibles for many reasons. Discovering their exquisite esthetic appeal has been our motivating factor. Investment value during inflationary times has been the rationale of others. Still others find paperweights, their history and acquisition, an intellectual challenge. Some find paperweights a unique gift selection. Whatever your reasons are for collecting paperweights, we are always available to help you build an outstanding collection. Your letter or phone call regarding the esthetics, identification, investment potential or gift selection will be promptly and enthusiastically answered. With this catalogue, we express our personal dedication to paperweight collecting and hope to encourage your interest in this very special field.

Sincerely,

Lawrence H. Selman

TABLE OF CONTENTS

SOME FACTS
ABOUT PAPERWEIGHTS

What is a collector's paperweight?

A collector's paperweight is a work of art. Its rich simplicity is crafted from the beauty and brilliance of glass. Although its shape (a hemisphere) and size (less than 4″) are somewhat standardized, the concepts and techniques within those boundaries are limited only by the imagination of the artist.

Despite the fact that its name connotes an item of utilitarian purpose, the glass paperweight has become, functionally and traditionally, a vehicle of artistic expression. With its origins reaching into ancient Egypt, this particular form of expression spans the centuries, reaching a zenith of beauty and technique during a fifteen-year period in the mid-nineteenth century. For reasons that are still highly speculative, the art seemed to lay dormant for nearly a century until the current renaissance in which the glassmaker's art is focused once more on these delightful objects. Seemingly lost or forgotten esoteric techniques are being rediscovered; contemporary makers are adding their own distinct creativity and ingenuity, and a new excitement prevails throughout the field.

Why should I collect paperweights?

Paperweights offer the collector the joy of discovery, beauty in miniature, and investment value. Your collection can be built on contemporary annual editions or select, authentic antique finds within your price range. Paperweights are lustrously timeless, colorfully enigmatic, and require little space or special care to display and enjoy. Private collectors, museums and corporations have seen a meteoric rise in the value of this art form and continue to enthusiastically invest in paperweights. You, too, can experience the discovery, beauty and investment potential of a paperweight collection.

What are some suggestions for the beginning collector?

The beginning collector should become thoroughly familiar with the history of paperweight production and types by reading the available literature. Especially helpful is the onsight inspection of paperweight collections at museums, galleries and, if possible, in private homes. Acquaint yourself with the classic producers, and then investigate the many available sources. Once you have read about and seen antique and contemporary weights, decide which weights appeal to you most, and why. There are paperweight designs and prices to meet every taste, purpose and pocketbook.

For the beginning paperweight collector we suggest the less expensive "J" Glass, Perthshire or Scotia weights. From there, you may want to add the limited annual editions from Baccarat, St. Louis, and American studio artists. Baccarat and d'Albret make fine sulphides and pose a challenge to the collector in obtaining a complete set. Acquiring an example from each of the classic manufacturers, Baccarat, Clichy and St. Louis, is an ideal way to begin your antique collection. Quality and taste, rather than quantity, are the key considerations in developing a paperweight collection.

How can I determine the authenticity of a paperweight?

An expert's opinion is the most reliable way to determine the authenticity of a paperweight. The next best way is to carefully research the weight in question by referring to many available reference sources. Do this *before* you purchase any weight. Be wary of high priced, fake French "originals."

Is there a national organization and periodical for paperweight collectors?

Yes, the Paperweight Collectors' Association is the formal organization founded in 1954 by Paul Jokelson. It has a current membership of 3500 collectors and publishes an annual bulletin containing articles on rare paperweights, special collections, reports on PCA conventions, artists and factories.

Where should I buy paperweights?

You should buy paperweights from a paperweight specialist who is constantly in touch with all the phases of paperweight collecting. Outside expertise is most important to the novice collector since it helps him buttress his own individual judgment. You can occasionally find "good buys" at antique shops and flea markets; however, remember *caveat emptor.*

L.H. Selman Limited is most willing to assist you in learning more about paperweights. We have been active in the paperweight field since 1968, promoting and offering our clients the best of the contemporary artists and studios, as well as the finest in antique weights. We have also published *Paperweights for Collectors*, the first comprehensive reference book for collectors. Appraisal services are available to all our collectors. We have recently appraised the Arthur Rubloff Collection of 1100 weights, now a permanent exhibit at the Art Institute of Chicago, the Doheny Collection in Camarillo, California, and the Fowler Collection in Los Angeles. We offer a complete selection of quality antique and contemporary paperweights, backed with years of experience and education in the field with individuals, corporations and museums numbering as our satisfied clients. We look forward to helping you, too, build an outstanding collection.

BOOKS AND
ACCESSORIES

A. PAPERWEIGHTS FOR COLLECTORS

Paperweights for Collectors, *in its third printing, is a comprehensive over-
view of important glassmakers of the classical period and also of present-day
factories and artists. The beautifully illustrated text includes important
sections on identification, paperweight production methods and new directions
in the field. Each section is generously illustrated with magnified and near-
life-size photographs—most in color. A glossary of terms and a helpful guide
to collecting is also included.* Paperweights for Collectors, *by Lawrence
H. Selman and Linda Pope-Selman, has been described by* Collector's News
as "an excellent book, beautifully photographed and printed," and by
American Collector *as "just about everything anybody could want to know
about antique or contemporary paperweights." This book is a must for a
basic reference library. Temporarily out of print. Enlarged and revised edition
due shortly.*

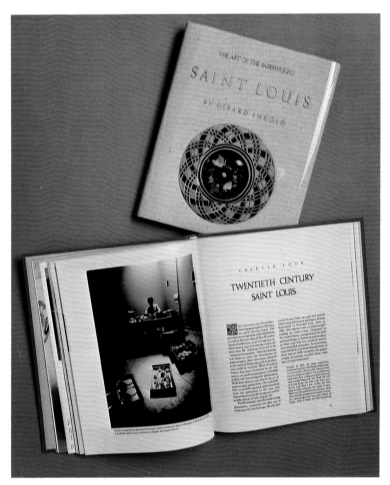

B. THE ART OF THE PAPERWEIGHT: SAINT LOUIS

This magnificently illustrated history of Saint Louis paperweights is the first in a series by Paperweight Press to chronicle the outstanding contemporary paperweight manufacturers. The text was thoughtfully prepared by Gérard Ingold, the Commercial Director of Saint Louis and edited by Lawrence H. Selman and Linda Pope-Selman.

The Saint Louis Archives graciously provided information and illustrations of the company's early and classic paperweight history. The book also features the collectors who kept the interest in paperweights alive during the years (1865-1952) when manufacturing had ceased. Of special note is the well-illustrated chapter on the processes involved in paperweight production. The book concludes with a catalogue, complete with full color photographs, of every limited edition since 1970.

Superb photography and a definitive text make this book invaluable to every collector of Saint Louis and other fine paperweights. The first edition is limited to 3,000 numbered copies. Hardbound, $49.50.

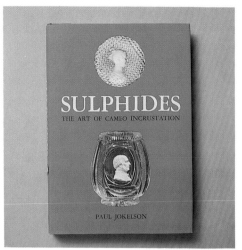

C. SULPHIDES, THE ART OF CAMEO INCRUSTATION

Paul Jokelson presents a thorough treatise on the specialized aspect of paperweight art involving the encasing of cameos in crystal. The 159 page book is lavishly illustrated and has its own protective slipcase. Clothbound edition, $9.00.

D. PAPERWEIGHTS: "FLOWERS WHICH CLOTHE THE MEADOWS"

The Corning Museum of Glass 1978 paperweight exhibition is pictorially documented with an accompanying text by Paul Hollister in this catalogue from the exhibit. Full color and real-life-size photographs of each weight in the show are featured in this 168 page publication. Hardbound, $30.00. Softbound, $25.00.

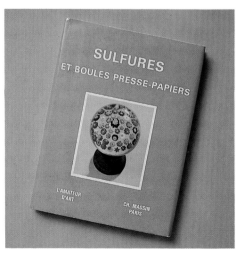

E. SULFURES ET BOULES PRESS-PAPIERS

Small, but informative, this guide by Edith Mannoni to paperweights and paperweight related objects is written in French and packed with full color photographs. $15.00

F. GLASS PAPERWEIGHTS AT OLD STURBRIDGE

One in a series on Old Sturbridge Village Massachusetts, this book by Paul Hollister examines the J. Cheney Wells collection, gives a brief history of paperweights and describes paperweight manufacturing procedures. Within the 52 pages are black-and-white photographs of each weight in the collection. $3.50

G. ANNUAL BULLETIN OF THE PAPERWEIGHT COLLECTORS' ASSOCIATION

This carefully edited bulletin by Paul Jokelson is issued annually and includes articles on rare paperweight finds, special collections, PCA conventions, artists and factories. Back issues for 1975 and 1977 are available, $15.00. 1978, 1979 and 1980, $20.00.

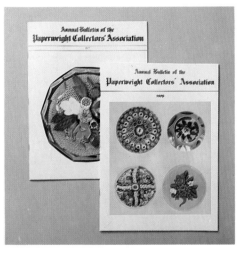

H. CORNING EXHIBITION JIGSAW PUZZLE

The Corning Museum of Glass has authorized their poster design to be used as a jigsaw puzzle of over 600 interlocking pieces. When assembled, this colorful, family fun activity measures 18" x 24". $7.95

The Corning Museum of Glass

Paperweights: "Flowers which clothe the meadows" April 29-Oct 21, 1978

I. CORNING PAPERWEIGHT EXHIBITION POSTER

This poster from the Corning Museum exhibition is 21" x 34" and shows thirty-six paperweights in full color. This illustration can give only an approximate idea of the breathtaking vividness of the poster. We think you will want one for yourself and one for a friend as an introduction to the art and beauty of paperweights. The quality of the poster makes it eminently suitable for framing. It will brighten up a wall anywhere. $7.50

J. MAHOGANY DISPLAY CABINET

A fine piece of traditional furniture, crafted of lustrous hand-rubbed mahogany , this display cabinet is adaptable to any home decor or commercial display. The warmth of fine wood, embellished by a single patterned inlay and made secure with a solid brass lock and key, surrounds your collectibles. Top lighting and a mirrored back provide maximum reflection for your favorite pieces. The adjustable glass shelves, with mounting brackets included, allow for flexible spacing. The dimensions are 29" x 29" x 7½". The case is suitable for the display of ivories, miniatures, netsukes, paperweights, perfumes or snuffboxes. Allow six to eight weeks for delivery. $660.00

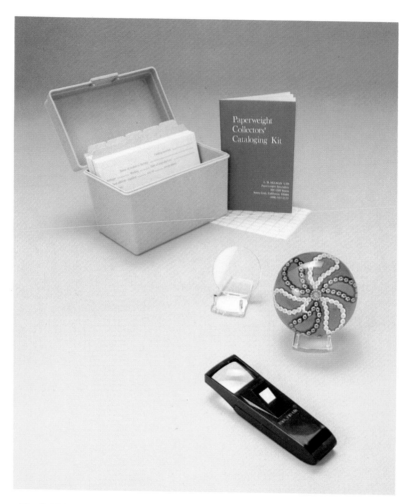

K. CATALOGING KIT

This kit of printed catalogue cards, self-adhesive labels, an information hand-book and a file box is for beginners or seasoned collectors. It simplifies cata-loguing and record keeping and thus furthers the enjoyment of your collection. It provides a handy, fingertip reference for insurance records and verifications of authenticity. $10.00

L. LUCITE PAPERWEIGHT STANDS

These lucite stands display large and small paperweights alike at just the right angle with balanced support. Minimum order of six stands, $15.00. *Each additional stand,* $2.50.

M. SELF-LIGHTED MAGNIFIER

For close inspection of the intricate details of paperweights, this handheld, self-lighted magnifier is invaluable. Batteries are included with the magnifier.

$4.50

CONTEMPORARY PAPERWEIGHTS

RICK AYOTTE

Rick Ayotte uniquely features birds as the subject matter of his naturalistic paperweights. His interest in ornithology and skill and experience as a scientific equipment glassworker have been fused into paperweight artistry since 1976. Paul Stankard inspired Rick to specialize in bird motifs in their natural habitat. Many of Rick's models flit about his backyard in Nashua, New Hampshire, where he lives with his wife and two children.

Rick Ayotte's lampwork paperweights are in editions of twenty-five to seventy-five pieces. Each weight is engraved with "Ayotte," the number of the weight and the year.

1. RICK AYOTTE

Superb colors and an unusual subject make this blue and gold Macaw one of our favorite Ayotte weights. This opaque green ground weight is signed in script on the side and is limited to 50 pieces. $250.

2. RICK AYOTTE

A Chickadee appears at home on a pine branch finely executed by Rick Ayotte. This compound weight is signed in script on the base. $400.

3. RICK AYOTTE

An old tree stump provides a resting place for a Hawk Owl silhouetted against the moonlit sky. The weight is signed in script on the base and is part of an edition of 75. $350.

4. RICK AYOTTE

A bright yellow Goldfinch with character-istic black and white markings is set in sparkling crystal. The Ayotte signature appears in script on the base. $225.

5. RICK AYOTTE

A translucent green ground adds to the camouflaging effect of the leafy branches which hide a Woodthrush. This unusual and handsome compound weight is signed by the artist in script on the base. $350.

6. RICK AYOTTE

Two leafy branches provide a place to rest for these Eastern Bluebirds. Signed in the usual manner, this compound weight is limited to 25 pieces. $400.

7. RICK AYOTTE

A *realistically modeled Baltimore Oriole with a vivid red body and striking black markings is captured in glass as he sits on a leafy acorn branch.* $250.

8. RICK AYOTTE

Ornithologically correct, this Herring Seagull is handsomely set against an opaque sky-blue background. Ayotte's signature appears on the base of this edition, which is limited to 75 pieces. $250.

9. RICK AYOTTE

This attractive compound weight features a House Wren amidst leaves and bushes within sparkling clear crystal. Part of an edition of 50, it is signed in script on the base. $400.

BACCARAT

*I*n 1953, Baccarat became the first modern factory to attempt cameo incrustation in paperweights. This revival was encouraged by Paul Jokelson, collector and paperweight connoisseur, and soon after, Baccarat produced a cameo of Queen Elizabeth II of England to commemorate her coronation. For almost twenty years, Baccarat has produced some of the finest limited edition sulphide paperweights.

In addition to sulphide paperweights, Baccarat includes millefiori and lampwork weights in their limited editions. The Gridel series, which features various animal silhouette canes among patterned millefiori motifs, has been a popular revival of a nineteenth century design.

Most Baccarat sulphide weights are inscribed on the edge of the bust with the artist's name, the year the sculpture was created and the name of the subject. Appearing on all Baccarat weights is an acid-etched seal of the company which includes the words "Baccarat, France" and the outlined forms of a goblet, decanter and tumbler. An interior date/signature cane and the number of the item are often included in special limited edition weights.

10. MODERN BACCARAT

From the Gridel series, the dividing spokes of this attractive panel weight feature all eighteen animal silhouettes. The motif is centered on a large deer silhouette cane. This weight was issued in a limited edition of 350 and is signed and dated. $225.

11. MODERN BACCARAT

Sculpted by Albert David, this handsome sulphide of John F. Kennedy is set against a deep blue ground. A red and white double overlay is faceted to reveal the subject. It is limited to 308 pieces and is signed in the usual manner. $500.

12. MODERN BACCARAT

A stylized garden snake peers whimsically out of this weight with a speckled rock ground. The date and the factory initial appear in a cane contained within the design. This weight is part of an edition of 300 pieces. $500.

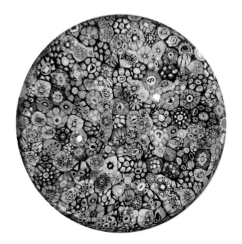

13. MODERN BACCARAT

This close pack millefiori weight contains a colorful and varied assortment of complex canes. All the signs of the zodiac in silhouette are interspersed within the motif, which is signed and dated and limited to 300 pieces.
$345.

14. MODERN BACCARAT

American President Woodrow Wilson as sculpted by M. Renard was issued in 1972 in an edition of 2400. The attractive translucent blue ground is enhanced by star-cutting. It is signed in the usual manner. *$60.*

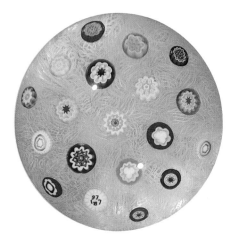

15. MODERN BACCARAT

A colorful assortment of millefiori canes is featured in this scattered millefiori weight with a lacy ground. It is signed and dated in one of the canes. *$260.*

16. MODERN BACCARAT

Two attractive stylized flowers with several buds and long graceful leaves form a pleasing arrangement set against a swirling white latticinio ground. Signed and dated in a cane near the base of the stem, this is a limited edition of 300. $312.

17. MODERN BACCARAT

The largest sulphide issued to date, this Mt. Rushmore commemorative is also the only oval sulphide produced so far. The cameo is attractively encased in a red and white double overlay, and is limited to 1000 pieces. $400.

18. MODERN BACCARAT

Superbly executed, this deep red "American Beauty" rose rests on a swirling white latticinio ground. Signed and dated in a millefiori cane near the base of the stem, this is a limited edition of 300. $475.

RAY AND ROBERT BANFORD

*R*ay and Robert Banford, father and son, both began making French style paperweights in 1971. They share a workshop and each other's know-how, but function as individual craftsmen. Ray's interest in paperweights was initiated by his wife's insistence to accompany her to the Corning Museum of Glass. Later, he was so fascinated by watching a glassmaker in action that he bought the entire stock and equipment of the elderly artisan. Paperweights, buttons and pendants are his glassmaking specialties.

Bob began his glassmaking career with a torch, a graduation gift from his parents. He made spun glass ships and carousels before creating limited edition paperweights. Bob works in complex lampwork motifs including florals, insects and reptiles. His work is displayed at Wheaton Village, the Corning Museum of Glass and the Smithsonian Institution.

Bob signs his weights with a red, white and blue "B" initial cane. Ray, his father, uses the same initial cane, but in different color combinations.

19. BOB BANFORD

A beautiful stylized dahlia in shades of pink
with an upright stamen cane, two buds and
abundant green foliage form an attractive
composition in clear crystal enhanced by a
star-cut base. Bob Banford's signature cane
is enclosed within the weight. $450.

20. BOB BANFORD

A lovely deep pink clematis and bud attract
a hovering dragonfly. The motif is set on a
pale opaque turquoise ground. The weight is
signed in a cane with the letter ''B'' for Bob
Banford. $450.

21. RAY BANFORD

This striking stylized rose and complementary
bud are dramatically enhanced by an unusual
fancy-cut base. The faceted weight is signed
in the usual Ray Banford manner. $450.

22. RAY BANFORD

A happy Cardinal guards her three delicate eggs set in a charming basket which rests precariously on a leafy branch. A Ray Banford initial cane signs the weight. $400.

23. BOB BANFORD

This kindly serpent apparently has an interest in upright blue flowers. The sunny yellow ground sets off the whole motif. A cane bears the Bob Banford initial. $350.

24. RAY BANFORD

A quartet of sun-ripened pears forms a distinguished composition set against parallel strips of white lacy cane. By Ray Banford, it is signed in a cane. $400.

25. RAY BANFORD

Two three-dimensional iris blooms and one bud are set on long slender stems with subtle iridescent coloring. This beautiful design is set in clear crystal and is star-cut for additional sparkle. Ray Banford's signature cane appears near the base of the stem. $450.

26. BOB BANFORD

Overall faceting enlivens an already elegant crimson flower and bud motif, set against a beautiful translucent blue ground. It is signed in a cane by Bob Banford. $400.

27. BOB BANFORD

The fancy-cut base gives the illusion of a basket within which floats a bright blue double clematis. A tiny bumblebee visits the bloom. Bob Banford signs the weight in a millefiori cane. $500.

D'ALBRET

In 1918, Roger Witkind organized the Cristalleries et Verreries de Vianne in Viannes, France. In 1967, Paul Jokelson, president of the Paperweight Collectors' Association, inspired the factory to inaugurate a series of sulphide paperweights under the name of "Cristalleries d'Albret."

D'Albret sulphides are produced in both regular and overlay editions. All weights of the same subject are finished with identical faceting and the same color or color combination. The base of each weight is acid-etched with a circle of cursive letters reading "CR. D'ALBRET-FRANCE." In addition, each sulphide is signed on the edge of the bust with the name of the subject, the date the sculpture was made and the initials of the artist.

Complete list of D'Albret sulphides in stock available upon request.

28. CRISTALLERIES D'ALBRET

Sculpted by Gilbert Poillerat, this portrait of Mark Twain is set against a beautiful translucent blue ground. Faceted overall, it was issued in an edition of 1000 pieces. $80.

29. CRISTALLERIES D'ALBRET

From a sculpture by Leo Holmgren, this cameo portrait of H. M. Gustaf VI was issued in a limited edition of 1000 pieces. $70.

30. CRISTALLERIES D'ALBRET

A sulphide of John J. Audubon by Gilbert Poillerat is attractively set against an electric blue ground. Faceted overall, it is limited to 1000 pieces. $75.
Overlay edition, not pictured. $170.

"J" GLASS

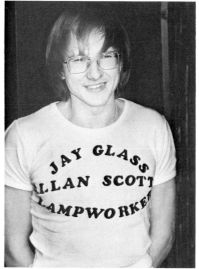

"J" Glass, a new Scottish factory in Crieff, Perthshire, is now in its second year of business. It derives its name from an enigmatic "J" signature cane found in certain nineteenth century Bohemian weights. John Deacons, "J"'s founder, is an experienced and skilled designer who was trained at the Edinburgh College of Art and later employed by Perthshire Paperweights.

"J" Glass paperweights are produced in classic millefiori motifs using authentic nineteenth century colors; the weights also feature lampwork motifs with floral, insect and reptilian subjects. Twelve separate editions for the United States were produced in 1980. Each edition contains not more than 101 pieces; one is retained by John Deacons. A blue "J" encircled by the year of manufacture in red, green and blue serves as the official signature/date cane. A numbered certificate, which describes the weight and is signed by John Deacons, accompanies each paperweight.

31. "J" GLASS

Six pretty clematis blossoms form a romantic garland set simply in sparkling crystal. The weight is limited to 101 pieces and is signed with a "J" cane. $260.

32. "J" GLASS

A brilliant pink wild rose with stylized leaves rests on a background of white latticinio spokes. The factory initial cane appears on the bottom of this weight, which is part of an edition of 101 pieces. $185.

33. "J" GLASS

Reminiscent of classic Baccarat flowers, this wine colored Royal primrose and bud is sure to enhance any collection. The signature cane is contained within the garland of purple and white canes which attractively surrounds the motif. This weight is part of an edition of 101. $240.

34. "J" GLASS

Reminiscent of antique Baccarat flowers, this pretty ruffle-edge primrose is set simply and elegantly in clear crystal. This is one in an edition of 101 pieces and is signed in a cane bearing the factory initial. $165.

35. "J" GLASS

A two-color latticinio swirl forms a dynamic background for a stylized bouquet of clematis-like flowers with star cane centers. This weight is signed on the bottom in the usual manner and is part of a limited edition of 101. $175.

36. "J" GLASS

"A rose is a rose," or so the saying goes, but this elegant old-fashioned rose by John Deacons is a knockout. Delicate millefiori canes in beautiful pastel colors surround the bloom and matching bud to create a romantic vision. The signature cane appears within the garland. This weight is limited to 101 pieces.
$260.

37. "J" GLASS

White latticinio twists alternate with red and green, and blue and yellow ribbons in this four-color crown weight topped with a large mille-fiori cane. This weight is signed in the usual manner and is limited to 101 pieces. $185.

38. "J" GLASS

Almost a valentine in glass, this pretty flash overlay is faceted to reveal a bouquet of sky-blue flowers on an upset muslin ground. Signed in the usual manner, this weight is part of a limited edition of 101. $300.

39. "J" GLASS

Two chains of delicate millefiori canes inter-twine, forming a garland, which encircles a petite butterfly on a purple-blue color ground. Fancy faceting adds visual interest to this limited edition of 101. The signature cane appears on the bottom. $325.

40. "J" GLASS

A graceful dragonfly hovers over a bouquet of fanciful flowers set in sparkling crystal. Faceting adds to the overall effect of this weight, which is limited to 101 pieces, and is signed in the usual manner. $325.

41. "J" GLASS

Two anemone blooms with cupped petals and numerous green leaves form a striking arrangement enhanced by a translucent blue ground. This limited edition is signed and dated J 1980. $150.

42. "J" GLASS

This "J" Glass version of the classic pansy motif is every bit as attractive as its antique counterpart. The signature cane is contained within the garland of delicate canes which encircle the flower. Limited to 101 pieces, this "J" Glass favorite is faceted overall. $240.

43. "J" GLASS

Delicate pastel millefiori canes form an enchanting interlaced garland motif in sparkling crystal. Faceted with five side windows and one large top window, this weight is signed in a cane with the factory initial. $110.

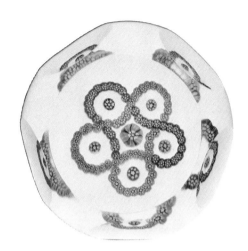

44. "J" GLASS

A fantasy botanical interpretation of spring wildflowers is displayed dramatically against an elegant black ground. A cane bearing the factory initial is set in the base of this limited edition of 101 pieces. $325.

45. "J" GLASS

A dainty upset muslin ground forms a pretty backdrop for two interlaced garlands of complex millefiori canes. Color combinations vary. Each weight in this limited edition of 101 is signed with the date of manufacture and the factory initial. $150.

46. "J" GLASS

A beautiful dahlia on a translucent blue ground features distinctive cupped petals. The bloom is set on a long stem with six green leaves. It is signed in a cane J 1980, and is limited to 101 pieces. $150.

47. "J" GLASS

This amber colored double clematis with two buds entwined about the base of the stem is attractively displayed on a translucent ruby colored ground. The weight is signed and limited to 101 pieces. $150.

48. "J" GLASS

Named a "Bloom in May," this bright yellow flower is complemented by slender green leaves. The motif rests on a translucent blue ground. Limited to 101 pieces, it is signed in the usual manner. $150.

49. "J" GLASS

Vivid blue and white petals centered on a
complex millefiori cane compose this stylized
primrose. The flower and matching bud are
set in clear crystal. Part of on edition of 101
pieces, this weight is signed and dated in a
millefiori cane. $150.

50. "J" GLASS

Reminiscent of a lace doily, this patterned
millefiori weight is composed of seven large,
identical millefiori canes. The motif, which
is signed in a cane bearing the factory initial,
is handsomely displayed on an unusual black
ground. This weight is limited to 101 pieces.
Colors may vary. $150.

51. "J" GLASS

A delicate white latticinio cushion forms a
romantic setting for three pastel-hued flowers.
Signed and dated J 1980, this weight is res-
tricted to 101 pieces. $150.

CHARLES KAZIUN

C harles Kaziun is a veteran glass artist. He has innovated a one-man method of millefiori cane production and is an expert at making muslin and swirling latticinio. Besides millefiori paperweights, Kaziun employs his creative genius by producing a variety of floral motifs such as the pansy, lily, dogwood and morning glory. Gold foil inclusions are another one of his specialties. Perfume bottles, footed miniature weights and buttons are also part of his creative output. Kaziun weights are signed with either a 14 karat gold "K" and/or a millefiori "K" signature cane worked into the design.

52. CHARLES KAZIUN

A beautiful interpretation of the Pansy motif
rests on a stunning opaque yellow ground. A
gold bee appears on one of the leaves. The
weight is signed on the reverse. $1100.

53. CHARLES KAZIUN

This miniature pedestal weight features an
upright Spider Lily on an opaque color ground
flecked with gold. The weight is signed with
a gold 'K' on the base. $375

54. CHARLES KAZIUN

Six large, complex canes surround a central
cane bearing an initial K. This patterned
millefiori weight is set on a blue ground.
                                   $650.

DAVID LOTTON

*D*avid Lotton is full of youthful optimism and possesses an open mind. Though he is only twenty, he has had several years of paperweight experience in the guild tradition as his father's assistant. tant. Charles, David's father, has been a successful artisan of the past decade, and now concentrates his efforts in the creation of vases.

Probably the most unique feature of David's weights are their vibrant colors and charming designs, perfect paperweight gift qualities. All of his weights carry his etched signature and the date on the base. The floral weights are numbered, and each edition consists of three hundred pieces.

From the small building behind his home in Lynwood, Illinois, David Lotton, assisted by a devoted assistant, Mrs. David Lotton, produces his personally favored floral weights. The ever improving quality and technique of these paperweights makes David Lotton an artist with a future.

55. DAVID LOTTON

At once both iridescent and transparent, this delightful "Dua Flora" weight is signed, dated and numbered in script on the base.
$100.

56. DAVID LOTTON

This intriguing iridescent weight features a graceful vine with flowers of millefiori canes. A signature and date appear in script on the base.
$60.

57. DAVID LOTTON

This limited edition of 300 features two pretty pink flowers on a graceful vine. Also in the "Dua Flora" series, this clear encased weight is signed, dated and numbered on the base.
$100.

LUNDBERG STUDIOS

James Lundberg has been the major force in developing this studio in a small town south of San Francisco. With a degree in art and European post graduate study in glass, James began producing weights for L.H. Selman in 1972. The studio consists of several artists operating in the Renaissance tradition, each contributing his special skill in creating iridescent Tiffany-style paperweights, vases, and jewelry, as well as clear weights. Seascapes, astronomical designs, birds, butterflies and flowers are popular Lundberg motifs, full of color and swirling suspension. James' intent is "to catch the splendor of the natural world in glass: either in a very literal way . . . or being merely suggestive. Glass is the only material (with integrity) capable of simulating nature."

Each Lundberg piece is signed with the studio name, artist's name, date and serial number. As of July, 1980, all Lundberg glass items are accompanied by a certificate of authenticity.

58. LUNDBERG STUDIOS

This ruffle-edge pansy on a graceful stem with a bud and deeply veined green leaves shows excellent lampwork technique. It is set on a pale iridescent ground and is signed in script on the base.   *$135.*

59. LUNDBERG STUDIOS

Delicate green millefiori canes suggest long strands of seaweed through which swims a whimsical fish and many stylized jellyfish. The motif is set against a deep-blue ground. A signature in script appears on the base.
$135.

60. LUNDBERG STUDIOS

Pink millefiori canes and deeply veined leaves combine to form a graceful flowering branch. A dainty butterfly floats above the pale ground, which sparkles with a subtle iridescence. The factory signature appears on the base. $135.

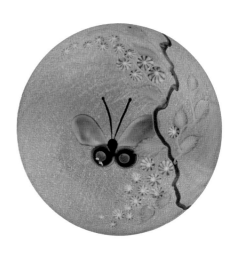

WILLIAM MANSON

W illiam Manson has had an excellent education in glass since the age of fifteen when he joined the Caithness Glass Company of Scotland. He was an apprentice to Paul Ysart, and when Ysart left Caithness to work on his own, Manson took over as the designer of limited editions for Caithness. In 1979, he opened his own studio south of Glasgow, Scotland. Especially unusual are his reptile and fish designs which are forever enclosed in their natural habitats. His weights are signed in the glass with a signature/date cane, and each is numbered on its base. Each design has been limited to 150 pieces.

61. WILLIAM MANSON

Two elegant white swans appear to float serenely on a deep blue pond. Classic in its simplicity, the entire motif is enclosed in a ring of delicate white millefiori canes. It is signed in the usual manner. $325.

62. WILLIAM MANSON

The rich coloring of this incredibly complicated lilac blossom is strikingly displayed against a deep-purple ground. Four graceful leaves complete the pleasing arrangement. The weight is signed. $350.

63. WILLIAM MANSON

A charming flower on a leafy stem is set on a beautiful translucent purple ground. The motif is enhanced by a garland of complex millefiori. Skillful faceting highlights the weight. This limited edition weight is signed by the artist. $300.

64. WILLIAM MANSON

This unusual weight provides us with an intimate view of the ocean's depths. A manta ray and a brightly colored fish may be seen cruising above the sandy bottom of the weight. This weight is both signed and limited to 150. $460.

65. WILLIAM MANSON

A ring of delicate and complex millefiori canes surrounds a well-executed, stylized flower set on a stem with four green leaves. The whole design rests on a translucent color ground. This limited edition of 150 is signed. $190.

66. WILLIAM MANSON

Perfected and captured in crystal, this stunning salamander has been painstakingly crafted to suggest the camouflaging ability of this legendary reptile in its natural habitat. This weight is signed in a cane and limited to 150 pieces. $570.

67. WILLIAM MANSON

Refreshing blue and white canes form a staved basket within which floats a pretty pink flower. An initial cane appears within the motif. $375.

68. WILLIAM MANSON

This cheerful "Elizabeth of Glamis Rose" with green leaves is set in the center of a garland of complex millefiori canes. The weight was produced in celebration of the 80th birthday of Her Majesty Queen Elizabeth, the Queen Mother. $390.

69. WILLIAM MANSON

A delicate butterfly with millefiori wings is surrounded by a garland of canes pulled down to form a staved basket. This weight is both signed and limited. $380.

MANSON/SCOTIA

Scotia of Scotland began in 1980 with nine editions of decorative and distinctive weights. Produced in the tradition of Paul Ysart by the workers in William Manson's glassworks, Scotia weights are an excellent starting point for beginning collectors. Millefiori canes in a variety of pleasant designs predominate Scotia's work; however, lampwork is also featured. The use of aventurine in the Dragonfly and Thistle editions is a unique element in these charming contemporary paperweights.

Perfect as gifts, Scotia weights measure three inches in diameter and are signed on the bottom with a thistle cane, the company's logo.

70. SCOTIA

Sure to please children of all ages, this Santa Claus motif is a nice way to say Merry Christmas. It is signed in a cane on the base. $120.

71. SCOTIA

This patterned millefiori weight features simple and complex millefiori canes in a spoke arrangement. The motif rests on an upset muslin cushion. The weight is signed in a cane. $150.

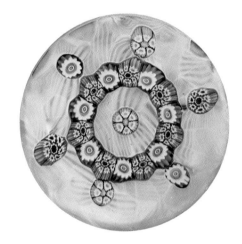

72. SCOTIA

Scotia presents winter as a snowman complete with scarf and stocking cap. The motif is set on a dark ground lit by a big yellow moon. The weight is signed. $120.

73. SCOTIA

This snowflake-patterned millefiori features many intricate canes which are displayed dramatically against a translucent blue ground. A signature cane appears on the base. $150.

74. SCOTIA

Scotia interprets the Scottish national flower, the thistle, by adding adventurine leaves and a thistle silhouette cane in the center of the bloom. The motif is encircled by a ring of millefiori canes and is signed on the base. $175.

75. SCOTIA

A fanciful fish rests on a blue and white jasper ground studded with eight millefiori canes. The weight is signed on the reverse with a thistle cane, the company logo. $120.

76. SCOTIA

Concentric rings of flower-like millefiori canes combine to give this pretty weight a classical look. It is signed with a thistle cane contained in the outer ring of canes. $150.

77. SCOTIA

The shiny adventurine body of this dragonfly suggests the iridescence of the real-life insect. A garland of delicate millefiori canes encircles the dragonfly. A signature cane bearing the factory logo may be found on the base. $175.

78. SCOTIA

Colorful and complex millefiori canes shine like bright stars against a translucent midnight-blue ground. A thistle cane bearing the factory signature signs the base. $150.

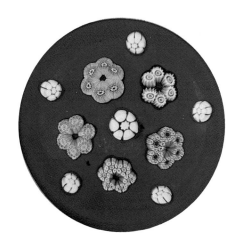

ORIENT AND FLUME

*D*rawing its name from bordering streets, Orient and Flume began operations in a small studio in Chico, California in 1972. A two-man effort at the outset, it now consists of nearly twenty persons, including artists, clerical, managerial and shipping personnel.

From its original line of vases, the output of the studio has been expanded to include not only paperweights, but lampshades, jewelry and stained glass.

As a cooperative studio, designs are developed by members of the staff who pool their ideas and incorporate them into the final product. While more cumbersome than other designing techniques, this team effort may account for the success of Orient and Flume . Their style is now uniquely their own.

Orient and Flume's early weights are characterized by art nouveau motifs, iridescence and surface decoration. Currently, they have combined art nouveau design elements with graceful traditional paper-weight techniques to create a distinctive modern style. Such basics as encasement, millefiori cane flowers, classic florals, butterflies and dragonflies are now included in their work.

Each Orient and Flume paperweight is signed, dated and numbered on the base and comes boxed with a certificate.

79. ORIENT AND FLUME

A dragonfly with fine latticinio wings hovers over an iridescent ground. Stylized cane flowers complete the motif, which is signed and limited to 250. $125.

80. ORIENT AND FLUME

The silhouette of a bird dominates the magnificent complex cane, the focal point of this pretty pastel mabrie weight. The weight is signed and dated on the base. Colors may vary. $150.

81. ORIENT AND FLUME

A small blue fish swims among the sea fronds in this underwater interpretation. This is part of a limited edition of 250 and is signed and dated on the base. $125.

PERTHSHIRE

*F*ounded in 1969, Perthshire Paperweights Limited of Crieff, Scotland, is dedicated to fine quality paperweights for all tastes and price ranges. Three different types of weights are made: special limited editions, limited to a certain number and produced only once; yearly limited editions, limited to a certain number, but produced annually; and unlimited editions, unlimited in number and produced annually.

All Perthshire weights are signed with one of three styles of signature/date canes. The yearly limited editions since 1969 contain an alphabet cane beginning with "A" for that year to "L" in 1980 embedded within the top design of the paperweight. Other weights carry a "P," the factory initial, cane with the year of manufacture either in the motif or on the bottom of the weight. And still others are identified by a single "P" cane within the top of the weight. (Recently, the artist's initials have been etched on the bottom of certain weights.)

82. PERTHSHIRE

A multicolored butterfly with cane wings is attractively displayed on a ribbed cushion ground, encircled by a garland of canes. The color of the ground will vary. The edition is limited to 450. $250.

83. PERTHSHIRE

This large triple swirl is in the style of antique Clichy weights. Signed and dated in the usual manner, the color combination used in the swirl will vary. $225.

84. PERTHSHIRE

A beautiful sculptured rose and bud are enhanced by overall faceting and a star-cut base. This weight, which is signed in a cane near the base of the stem, is part of an edition of 300 pieces. $395.

85. PERTHSHIRE

This charming miniature patterned millefiori motif is set on a translucent blue ground. The letter "L", representing the year 1980, appears in the center cane. This weight was produced in an edition of 500. $112.50.

86. PERTHSHIRE

The Christmas weight for 1980, this attractive red candle on a sprig of holly leaves is set on a fine white latticinio ground underlaid with either red, blue, or green. Signed and dated, it is limited to 300 pieces. $200.

87. PERTHSHIRE

This miniature weight contains a central flower motif surrounded by a series of leaves and three small millefiori canes, all on a color ground of either ruby or blue. This limited edition of 450 pieces is signed in the usual manner. $145.

88. PERTHSHIRE

This is a traditional style of weight containing a garland of canes on a white latticinio ground. In the loops formed by the garland are a series of colored silhouettes representing early forms of transport. It is limited to 400 and is signed in a millefiori cane. $200.

89. PERTHSHIRE

Issued in 1977 for the holiday season, the two bells in this weight are composed entirely of fine pink and white millefiori canes set on a superb translucent ruby ground. Limited to 325, this weight is faceted overall. $200.

90. PERTHSHIRE

This miniature weight contains a small colorful butterfly floating inside fancy-cut green and white double overlay. The weight is signed in a cane and is limited to 500 pieces. $250.

91. PERTHSHIRE

An attractive blue lampwork flower is surrounded by a series of delicate buds set on an amethyst color ground. The weight is overlaid in amethyst and is faceted. This weight is signed with the factory signature and is limited to 300 pieces. $450.

92. PERTHSHIRE

A basket of three-dimensional fruit containing a pear, an orange, a lemon, and a small group of plums complemented by green leaves rests in a latticinio basket. Signed and dated on the base, this weight is limited to 350 pieces. $500.

93. PERTHSHIRE

In this patterned millefiori weight, seven unusual silhouette canes are surrounded by beautiful green and blue complex canes. The whole motif is set on an opaque red ground. This weight is signed and limited. $300.

94. PERTHSHIRE

This charming patterned millefiori weight features a selection of complex millefiori canes alternating with latticinio spokes. The motif, which is centered on a sailboat cane, is underlaid with a muslin ground. This signed weight is limited to 300 pieces. $200.

95. PERTHSHIRE

A tiny circus seal balancing a ball on his nose is set within a translucent ruby overlay. This faceted weight is signed in the usual manner and is limited to 400 pieces. $320.

96. PERTHSHIRE

This patterned millefiori weight features a selection of closely set canes divided by latticinio twists in the manner of a checker board. This signed weight is limited to 250 pieces.
$155.

97. PERTHSHIRE

This patterned millefiori weight contains an assortment of colorful millefiori canes set on a translucent color ground. The factory initial cane appears within the motif. $45.

98. PERTHSHIRE

Scattered millefiori on lace features a variety of colorful and complex millefiori canes, including several silhouettes, all set on a cushion of finely spun latticinio threads. A cane bearing the factory signature is included within the motif. $115.

99. PERTHSHIRE

This medium size millefiori weight features the factory initial cane in the central floret. Colors will vary. $35.
Large size millefiori. $50.

100. PERTHSHIRE

A large millefiori weight featuring many colorful canes and twists is set on a clear ground. Within the motif is a cane bearing the factory initial. It is faceted on top with one large concave window. Colors will vary.
$90.

101. PERTHSHIRE

This attractive yearly limited edition features six large complex millefiori canes set in sparkling crystal. The center cane bears a letter indicating the year of manufacture. Faceted overall and star-cut on the base, it is a yearly limited edition.
$115.

102. PERTHSHIRE

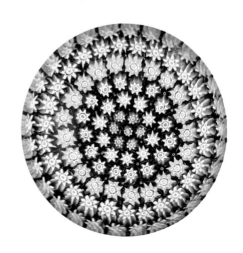

This close concentric millefiori weight contains a variety of multicolored canes set on a clear ground. The factory initial cane appears within the motif.
$45.

ST. LOUIS

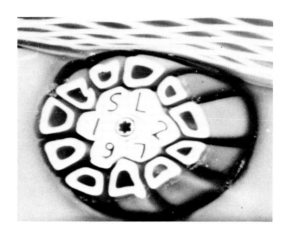

Cristalleries de St. Louis is one of the foremost glass factories in the world today. It resumed paperweight production in 1953 after an almost one hundred year hiatus. Most modern St. Louis weights are patterned after their superb nineteenth century classic designs. Millefiori, lampwork and sulphide techniques are employed in the many annual limited editions which have consistently been produced since 1970.

Ever faithful to the classic tradition, St. Louis produces mushroom overlay, marbrie, pinwheel and piedouche weights. Gold inclusion weights have been another St. Louis contemporary paperweight innovation. In addition to their annual edition paperweights, St. Louis also creates distinctive paperweight related items: candlesticks, newel posts, shot glasses and handcoolers. Modern St. Louis weights are signed with the initials "SL" and the date within a cane, and each weight is accompanied by a certificate of authenticity.

103. MODERN ST. LOUIS

This superb basket of flowers design was inspired by the famous antique Clichy weight. Beautiful millefiori canes represent tiny flowers, while latticinio and spiral twists suggest the basket. The edition is limited to 250 pieces.
$840.

104. MODERN ST. LOUIS

This gorgeous display of lampwork flowers is reminiscent of the rare Mt. Washington plaque produced in Massachusetts in the 1880s. It measures approximately 1½″ x 6¾″ x 4½″ and is limited to 25 pieces.
$2800.

105. MODERN ST. LOUIS

This stunning pink and white double overlay is cut with a graceful vine motif around the sides of the weight. A gilded, coiled lizard perches on top. Issued in a limited edition of 150 pieces, this weight is signed in a cane on the base.
$1,400.

106. MODERN ST. LOUIS

This sulphide weight commemorates the 1953 coronation of Queen Elizabeth II. Set on a deep blue ground, the regal sulphide portrait is surrounded by a garland of mille-fiori canes and is signed on the base. $350.

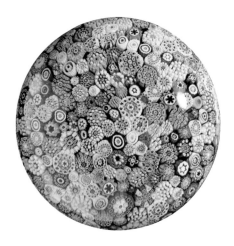

107. MODERN ST. LOUIS

Close millefiori. This classic weight again displays a selection of St. Louis' finest complex millefiori canes set closely together, forming an elegant overall arrangement and is limited to 250 pieces. $520.

108. MODERN ST. LOUIS

A distinguished cameo portrait of General de Gaulle is handsomely set in an opaque green ground. This weight is limited to 200 pieces and is faceted overall. $150.

109. MODERN ST. LOUIS

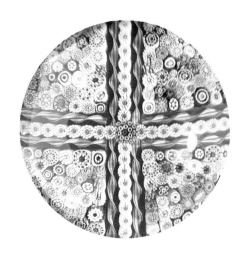

The cross motif is rare in antique weights. This weight features a selection of St. Louis' best millefiori canes which are divided into quadrants by a cross composed of identical canes bordered by latticinio twists. There are 250 pieces in this limited edition. $580.

110. MODERN ST. LOUIS

A charming grouping of many stylized flowers fills this weight, forming a colorful spring bouquet in sparkling crystal. There are 250 pieces in this limited edition.

$560.

111. MODERN ST. LOUIS

A handsome close concentric millefiori tuft forms the well-executed mushroom, which is enclosed within a pristine white and rich green double overlay. The edition is limited to 250 pieces. $700.

112. MODERN ST. LOUIS

The exceptionally vivid colors of the three-dimensional pears, plums and cherries stand out dramatically against the white latticinio basket in this faceted fruit weight. A limited edition of 250 pieces, it is signed and dated in a cane on the base. $390.

113. MODERN ST. LOUIS

A 24-karat gold medallion, inspired by the death mask of Tutankhamun, is set on either a beautiful opaque orange or turquoise ground and is surrounded by a garland of millefiori canes. It is limited to 300 pieces. $490.

114. MODERN ST. LOUIS

Three cherries and a ripe pear rest on a cushion of fine white latticinio. This miniature fruit weight is part of a limited edition of 250 and is signed in a millefiori cane on the base. $320.

115. MODERN ST. LOUIS

This weight captures the essence of love in color, symbol and word. Gazing whimsically at a garland of flowers, Cupid is love's classic image. Pretty lampwork flowers encircle the cameo motif bannered "Amour." It is limited to 400 pieces and is signed in the usual manner. $385.

116. MODERN ST. LOUIS

A gold foil inclusion portraying George Washington on horseback is set on an opaque blue ground accented by a grouping of mille-fiori stars. Faceted overall, this weight is limited to 250 pieces. $310.
The overlay edition is not pictured. $450.

117. MODERN ST. LOUIS

A fanciful blossom with five rounded cane petals on a stem with a bud and five green leaves is set on a cheerful opaque pistachio color ground. Signed and dated, this weight is limited to 250 pieces. $190.

PAUL STANKARD

*P*aul Joseph Stankard is in the vanguard of contemporary glass artists. His distinctive floral designs are meticulously crafted in botanical accuracy and display a dramatic sense of design and color. He has combined his scientific glassblowing skills with a keen interest in wild and domesticated flowers. Much of Paul's initial floral inspiration comes from the Blaschka Glass Models of Plants at Harvard University.

Stankard weights are uniquely contemporary in motif, featuring exceptionally fine detail and intricate patterns. Tiny blossoms, delicate stamens, veined leaves and variegated root systems distinguish his paperweights.

Stankard limited editions contain between twenty-five and seventy-five pieces. The early weights bear either an etched signature on the base or side, or an "S" or "PS" signature cane. Current Stankard weights are identified with an "S" signature cane placed at the base of a color ground or on the side of a clear ground.

118. PAUL STANKARD

Paul Stankard has captured the essence of a Blue Gentian in this marvelous weight. The weight is signed in the usual manner with Paul's initial cane. $800.

119. PAUL STANKARD

Botanically correct, "Wild Foxglove" features three stems of pristine white compound flowers, slender green leaves and an intricate root system displayed on a translucent blue ground. The weight is signed. $550.

120. PAUL STANKARD

Among Paul's most complex botanical creations, this Paphiopedilum Orchid, complete with the appropriate leaves and root system, is set in clear crystal. It is an experimental design and is signed with a "PS" cane. $800.

121. PAUL STANKARD

Dwarf Field Pansy features three delicate blossoms, two buds, a cluster of seeds and a complex root system. Signed and dated on the side, it is set against a beautiful translucent blue ground. $600.

122. PAUL STANKARD

A faceted floral profusion of fanciful flowers fills this fancy experimental weight, which is signed on a millefiori cane bearing the initials "PS." $1,000.

123. PAUL STANKARD

This delicate white Flax blossom and bud on a long stem is set on a rich opaque green ground. It is signed on the side with an "S" cane. $500.

124. PAUL STANKARD

This delicate Orchid is one of the species of flowers Paul Stankard does best. Graceful, yet complex and botanically faithful, this experimental weight is signed in a cane with the artist's initials. $700.

125. PAUL STANKARD

"Apple Blossoms," an exclusive limited edition produced for L. H. Selman Ltd., is nothing short of spectacular. This large weight was issued in a limited edition of twenty-five pieces and is signed in an initial cane on the side. $2000.

126. PAUL STANKARD

A pair of big, bright, Brown-eyed Susans on slender stalks with slim graceful leaves is set in sparkling clear crystal. This weight is signed by Paul in a cane and in script on the side. $600.

DELMO AND DEBBIE TARSITANO

*D*elmo and Debbie Tarsitano, father and daughter, share a great talent in creating paperweights with outstanding lampwork motifs. Delmo specializes in fruits, vegetables and reptiles, while Debbie creates stylized floral compositions. After collecting antique paperweights for several years, Delmo and Debbie began creating their own in 1978.

Their weights were included in the 1978 Corning Museum of Glass Exhibition, "Paperweights: 'Flowers which clothe the meadows.'" They pride themselves on their dimensional and realistic weights and hope to create entirely new designs as well as to conquer encasement techniques.

Tarsitano weights are produced in a very limited number and are neither dated nor numbered. Before 1980, their weights were signed with an initial cane which combined a "D" and a "T" in the form of a "D" cane. Their weights are now identified by a "DT" cane placed at the edge of the motif.

127. DEBBIE TARSITANO

A stylized Zinnia in a delicate pink hue offers a resting place for a realistically modeled bumblebee. Faceting and star-cutting further enhance the weight, which is signed with the initials "DT." $450.

128. DEBBIE TARSITANO

This wonderful flower explosion features a profusion of delicate and colorful blooms completely filling the large weight. The effect is simply breathtaking. Debbie Tarsitano's latest creation is surely her finest effort to date. $1500.

129. DELMO TARSITANO

Three large luscious strawberries combine with three pristine white blossoms amid abundant green leaves. This large, finely executed weight is no less than spectacular. $525.

130. DEBBIE TARSITANO

A quartet of brilliant yellow Marsh Marigolds with deeply veined emerald green leaves forms an elegant composition in clear crystal. It is signed by Debbie with an initial cane.
$450.

131. DEBBIE TARSITANO

Debbie's interpretation of the classical nosegay motif features a millefiori flower and one lampwork flower set on a stem with complementary foliage. The weight is signed in a cane at the base of the stem. $400.

132. DEBBIE TARSITANO

Surrounded by sparkling faceted crystal, this attractive Pansy and bud motif is superbly executed in Debbie Tarsitano's own inimitable style. It is signed in the usual manner. $400.

133. DELMO TARSITANO

Delmo Tarsitano has captured the essence of the peach so completely, you can almost feel the soft fuzz on these large fruits. The motif is set simply and effectively in sparkling clear crystal. $425.

134. DEBBIE TARSITANO

One of the most charming flower compositions yet produced by Debbie and christened "An English Garden," this pretty collection of blooms will brighten your paperweight garden year-round. $600.

135. DELMO TARSITANO

Three red ripe cherries on delicate stems decorate a leafy branch. The fancy faceting plays visual tricks and from some angles makes the design appear to be a whole tree full of fruit. $475.

136. DELMO TARSITANO

One large, very realistic pear demands attention. This fine creation is by Delmo Tarsitano and is signed in an initial cane.

$370.

137. DEBBIE TARSITANO

One of the most attractive floral bouquets ever created, this mix of fanciful flowers, set in clear crystal, is Debbie Tarsitano's best.

$450.

138. DEBBIE TARSITANO

Brilliant red Poppies set on a stem with several green leaves make up this simple yet elegant composition in clear crystal. The weight is signed with the initials "DT" in a single cane near the base of the stem. $350.

139. DELMO TARSITANO

Three Pepper blossoms and three Peppers make up this unusual creation set in clear crystal by Delmo Tarsitano. $370.

140. DELMO TARSITANO

By Delmo Tarsitano, these two ripe pears on a leafy branch form a distinctive arrangement in clear crystal. The base is star-cut and the weight is signed in a cane with Delmo's initials. $350.

141. DEBBIE TARSITANO AND PAUL YSART

Two fine paperweight artists have combined efforts to produce this charming floral motif. Debbie created the spotted Wheatflower and Paul created the complex millefiori canes which surround the bloom. $850.

VICTOR TRABUCCO

Victor Trabucco began producing paperweights in 1977 after having seen a few antique French weights in a local gift shop. Previous to that time, he had taught himself the art of lampwork, experimenting and reading as much as he could to perfect his art. Victor melts rods of crystal, a unique procedure in paperweight production, to use to encase his colorful floral arrangements. He also creates award winning glass sculptures in his basement studio in suburban Buffalo, New York.

Victor would like to further incorporate his sculpture techniques within his clean and color coordinated paperweights. He produces approximately 100-150 clear crystal enclosed weights per year. Each edition consists of twenty-five to seventy-five pieces. Victor's weights are signed with a "T" cane; his signature and the date are also etched on the side of each weight.

142. VICTOR TRABUCCO

A bouquet of spring Violets form an enchanting composition in sparkling crystal. Signed in script on the base, this weight is faceted with one top and five side windows. $300.

143. VICTOR TRABUCCO

The fish in this unusual motif from Victor Trabucco is just about to be reeled in. This faceted weight is signed in script on the side. $250.

144. VICTOR TRABUCCO

Bright and colorful, this mixed floral arrangement sparkles with Victor Trabucco's creativity. This weight is signed in the usual manner. $300.

145. VICTOR TRABUCCO

Many small Lavender buds on a stem and two additional leafy branches with delicate tendrils form an unusual and refreshing arrangement. The weight is signed and dated in script on the side of the weight. $200.

146. VICTOR TRABUCCO

A pair of vivid yellow Bellflowers stands out dramatically against a refreshing translucent blue ground. This weight is signed in the usual manner. $225.

147. VICTOR TRABUCCO

Two dainty pink flowers and three buds make a simple yet dramatic composition in clear crystal. It is signed and dated in script on the side. $200.

148. VICTOR TRABUCCO

A beautiful spray of Forget-me-nots is set in clear crystal. The weight is cut with five side and one top facets, adding visual interest to this dainty motif. It is signed in script on the base. $250.

149. VICTOR TRABUCCO

A charming bouquet of different flowers—Fuchsia, Forget-me-not, Bellflower—is set simply and elegantly amidst abundant foliage. This weight is signed in script on the base. $300.

150. VICTOR TRABUCCO

Two stylized Lavender blossoms and one half-opened bloom are combined with long slender leaves in clear crystal. The weight is signed in the usual manner. $200.

ANTIQUE
PAPERWEIGHTS

ANTIQUE FACTORIES

The classical period of paperweight manufacture is generally
considered to have extended from 1840 to 1860. The idea of
paperweights as a saleable art form is thought to have been introduced
in 1845 at the Austrian Industrial Fair in Vienna. In Vienna, Pietro
Bigaglia of Venice, one of a long line of Muranese glassworkers,
displayed his wares. It has been surmised that Bigaglia's works were
the catalyst for the subsequent sophisticated paperweight manufacturing techniques developed by the French.

Three outstanding French factories set the pace in the production
of paperweights. These were St. Louis, Baccarat, and Clichy. Also
prominent in the nineteenth century were the English factories of
Bacchus and Whitefriars.

The art migrated to the United States a decade or more after
1860, and continued to flourish until shortly after the turn of the
century. Significant American companies were The New England
Glass Company, Gillinder, Mt. Washington and later Millville.

The classical period of paperweights has given us an unequalled
legacy of beauty. In addition, its inspiration has given rise to new
present day heights in artistry and imagination.

151. ANTIQUE AMERICAN

The petals of this brilliant blue clematis are centered on a rabbit silhouette cane. Three deeply veined leaves complete the motif, which rests on a white latticinio ground.

$650.

152. ANTIQUE AMERICAN

Many colorful ribbons in a random sequence add an almost modern note to this antique American crown weight centered on a simple white cane. $825.

153. ANTIQUE AMERICAN

Four ripe pears are arranged symmetrically around a fifth fruit in this well-formed fruit-in-a-basket weight produced at the Sandwich Glassworks. Red cherries and emerald green leaves complete the pleasing composition.

$750.

154. ANTIQUE AMERICAN

Many colorful bits and pieces of millefiori canes and lacy twists are set in a jumbled array in this "end-of-day" or scrambled weight by the New England Glass Co. $150.

155. ANTIQUE AMERICAN

By the Sandwich Glass Co., this royal blue double clematis with its complementary foliage is attractively set on a swirling white latticinio cushion. $800.

156. ANTIQUE AMERICAN

This charming New England Glass Company patterned millefiori is a delight to the eye. Typical faceting highlights the pastel millefiori, which rest on a cushion of latticinio. $750.

157. ANTIQUE AMERICAN

A fine white latticinio cushion supports a rare patriotic upright bouquet with lampwork and millefiori cane flowers and surrounding foliage. The motif, which is set in clear crystal, is enhanced by overall faceting. $1750.

158. ANTIQUE AMERICAN

A pleasing selection of delicate canes is featured in this patterned millefiori weight from the New England Glass Company. The canes rest on a white latticinio cushion. $485.

159. ANTIQUE AMERICAN

Rare and unusual, this blue and white striped double clematis by the Sandwich Glass Company is set in clear crystal. $850.

160. ANTIQUE BACCARAT

Surrounded by deeply veined bright green leaves, this red and white primrose and bud arrangement is dramatically displayed within a circle of millefiori florets. $2350.

161. ANTIQUE BACCARAT

Fancy millefiori canes form the wings of this rare Baccarat butterfly. Star-cutting on the base adds sparkle to this colorful, winged insect, which is surrounded by a garland of florets. $2800.

162. ANTIQUE BACCARAT

Blue markings identify this lovely bloom as a Baccarat wheatflower, whose stamen is composed of arrowhead canes. The motif is set in clear crystal. $4500.

163. ANTIQUE BACCARAT

A superb salmon orange clematis rests on a cushion of upset muslin. The striking motif is encircled by a ring of typical Baccarat canes. $3250.

164. ANTIQUE BACCARAT

This fine example of a close pack millefiori motif contains a colorful array of typical Baccarat canes including silhouettes of a dog, man, rooster, deer, horse and elephant. This weight is signed and dated "B1847." $1650.

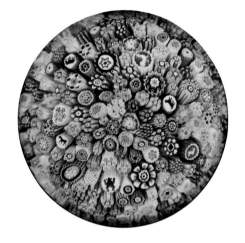

165. ANTIQUE BACCARAT

This rare floral bouquet is superb! It features a selection of charming flowers—three white clematis blossoms, a vivid red double clematis, and a classic pansy. The arrangement is set in clear crystal. $8500.

166. ANTIQUE BACCARAT

*A colorful selection of Baccarat's best mille-
fiori canes form the closely packed tuft in this
classic mushroom weight. A spiral torsade
with air rings above and below it encircles
the base.* $1150.

167. ANTIQUE BACCARAT

*A beautiful blue and white double overlay is
faceted to reveal two interlacing trefoil garlands. The delicate millefiori chains are centered on a smaller circular garland which
encloses a single complex floret.* $7400.

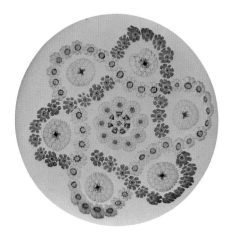

168. ANTIQUE BACCARAT

*Identical millefiori canes in blue and white
form interlacing trefoil garlands in this
striking patterned millefiori weight. This is
a piedouche weight with a salmon torsade.*
$2100.

169. ANTIQUE BACCARAT

This spectacular primrose features six vivid blue and white petals and eleven emerald green leaves. The star-cut bottom and overall faceting further enhance the weight. $1150.

170. ANTIQUE BACCARAT

This fabulous three-flower flat bouquet features a pansy, a double clematis and a primrose, so typical of Baccarat. This bouquet with complementary foliage is set in clear crystal. $7900.

171. ANTIQUE BACCARAT

This fine example of the classic Baccarat pansy features two large purple petals and three lower yellow petals edged and striped in purple. Green foliage and a bud complete the motif, which is accented by star-cutting on the base. $725.

172. ANTIQUE BACCARAT

This fine example of a rare shamrock and butterfly patterned millefiori is attractively set on a bed of upset muslin. $2950.

173. ANTIQUE BACCARAT

Handsome and rare, this clematis bud weight features blossoms in both pink and white. The unusual motif is set in clear crystal. $1600.

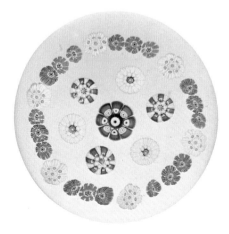

174. ANTIQUE BACCARAT

Vivid blue and white canes encircle seven complex florets in red and green in this pretty patterned millefiori weight. $650.

175. ANTIQUE BACCARAT

Bright and cheery, this unusual two-color clematis and its matching bud are surrounded by abundant bright green foliage. The attractive composition is set in sparkling clear crystal. $2500.

176. ANTIQUE BACCARAT

Animal silhouettes and colorful geometric canes are evenly dispersed on a lacy ground of upset muslin. This classic Baccarat weight is initialed and dated "B1848." $1650.

177. ANTIQUE BACCARAT

Two buds entwine about a central stalk which supports a rare yellow double clematis with a star-dust stamen cane. Abundant foliage completes the motif, which is set in clear crystal with decorative side facets. $2500.

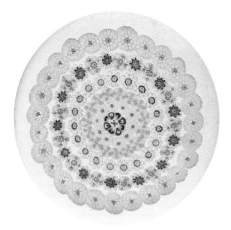

178. ANTIQUE BACCARAT

Delicate close concentric rings of typical Baccarat millefiori canes are centered on a complex arrowhead floret. The motif is set in clear crystal. $2100.

179. ANTIQUE BACCARAT

Composed of many brightly colored geometric canes so typical of Baccarat, this weight is perfect for beginning collectors to use as a frame of reference for identification. $500.

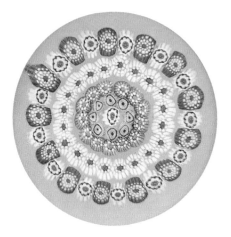

180. ANTIQUE BACCARAT

Four concentric garlands of complex canes make up this pretty patterned millefiori motif, which is set in clear crystal. $250.

181. ANTIQUE CLICHY

Refreshing in blue and white, the spokes of this well-formed swirl weight are centered on a white star-dust cane. $1600.

182. ANTIQUE CLICHY

An opaque white "sodden snow" ground dramatically displays a colorful looped garland motif. $950.

183. ANTIQUE CLICHY

An opaque apple-green color ground forms the backdrop for a pretty looped garland motif of delicate "pastry mold" canes. $950.

184. ANTIQUE CLICHY

A colorful selection of characteristic Clichy canes are set in a spaced concentric millefiori pattern. One rare and very untypical cane appears at the lower right as a 'C' signature cane. $950.

185. ANTIQUE CLICHY

Sparkling crystal sets off delicate garlands of millefiori florets in pretty pastel hues. Overall faceting further enhances the weight. $650.

186. ANTIQUE CLICHY

This beautiful scattered millefiori on lace features bright Clichy "pastry mold" canes about a central pink and green Clichy rose. $1050.

187. ANTIQUE CLICHY

An opaque apple-green color ground serves as a stunning backdrop for this patterned millefiori weight. The millefiori canes are set in five circlets about a large central pink cane. $1250.

188. ANTIQUE CLICHY

A delicate arrangement of beautiful pastel millefiori canes reminds one of a spring garden. The motif is set in sparkling clear crystal. $750.

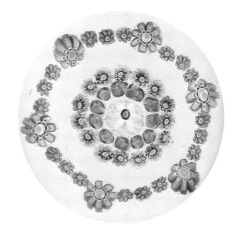

189. ANTIQUE CLICHY

A distinguished royal blue ground forms a beautiful background for this patterned millefiori motif centered on a pink and green Clichy rose. $850.

190. ANTIQUE CLICHY

The spokes of this dramatic three-color swirl radiate from a large green "pastry mold" cane. $2000.

191. ANTIQUE CLICHY

One delicate trefoil garland resembles a chain of tiny pink and green flowers. The garland weaves in and out of seven complex Clichy canes, including three Clichy roses. $800.

192. ANTIQUE CLICHY

This close concentric millefiori weight is filled with a spectacular assortment of Clichy's most famous canes—the edelweiss, moss, and Clichy rose. The millefiori motif is enclosed within a red and white staved basket. $4500.

193. ANTIQUE CLICHY

This superb spaced concentric millefiori weight features many famous Clichy canes on a rare green "moss" ground. $12,000.

194. ANTIQUE CLICHY

Four large pink and green Clichy roses dominate this breathtaking garland motif set on an eye-dazzling opaque turquoise ground. $2500.

195. ANTIQUE CLICHY

Many typical Clichy canes are divided checkerboard-fashion by white latticinio twists in this very pretty chequer weight. $1150.

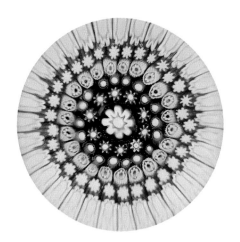

196. ANTIQUE ENGLISH

*Concentric rings of red, white, and blue florets
distinguish this Whitefriars patterned millefiori weight centered on a large white cane.*
$400. pair

197. ANTIQUE ENGLISH

*The date, 1848, is easily visible within the
ring of yellow canes in this close concentric
patterned millefiori weight by Whitefriars.*
$250.

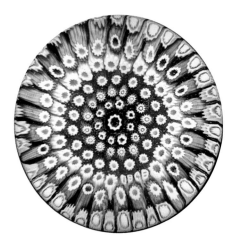

198. ANTIQUE ENGLISH

*This colorful close concentric millefiori is
by Whitefriars. The date, 1848, is contained
within one of the rings of bold geometric
canes.*
$440.

199. ANTIQUE ST. LOUIS

A *salmon-pink double clematis is the very essence of spring, displayed in sparkling clear crystal with a star-cut base.* $1350.

200. ANTIQUE ST. LOUIS

Stylized blossoms in various colors combine with bright green leaves within this bouquet, encircled by a beautiful white spiral torsade. The weight is further enhanced by multi-faceting. $2800.

201. ANTIQUE ST. LOUIS

Emerald green leaves surround a vivid blue double clematis with a distinctive, sharply serrated cane in the center of the bloom. A cushion of white latticinio threads completes the motif, which is faceted for added visual interest. $1200.

202. ANTIQUE ST. LOUIS

A jumbled array of bits and pieces of St. Louis canes and lacy twists makes a joyous abstract statement in crystal. This weight is referred to as a scrambled or end-of-day weight. $300.

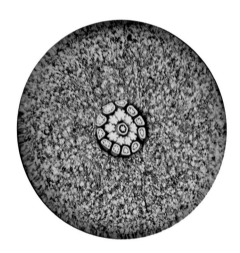

203. ANTIQUE ST. LOUIS

A single complex cane strikes an almost modern note when set simply in the center of this green and white jasper ground weight. $235.

204. ANTIQUE ST. LOUIS

A stunning deep pink dahlia accented by five emerald green leaves is set simply and elegantly in clear crystal. $2800.

205. ANTIQUE ST. LOUIS

A rich pink double clematis is set on a stem with five deeply serrated bright green leaves. The bloom rests on a swirling white latticinio ground. $900.

206. ANTIQUE ST. LOUIS

Cheerful red and green ribbons alternate with white latticinio twists in this well-formed crown weight. $1450.

207. ANTIQUE ST. LOUIS

A formal arrangement of pears and cherries sits primly in the center of a fine white latticinio ground in this mixed fruit assemblage from St. Louis. $1400.

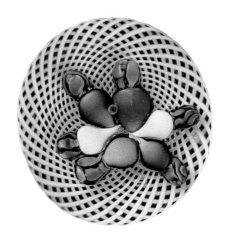

208. ANTIQUE ST. LOUIS

A colorful arrangement of turnips forms a refreshing still life displayed on a white latticinio cushion. $750.

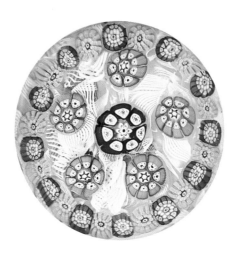

209. ANTIQUE ST. LOUIS

An upset muslin ground acts as a backdrop for the large complex canes in this handsome patterned millefiori weight. $750.

210. ANTIQUE ST. LOUIS

This spectacular weight features a pristine white pom-pom or camomile with bud and four deeply serrated green leaves on a rare pink latticinio cushion. $2600.

211. ANTIQUE ST. LOUIS

This brilliantly colored and well-formed purple dahlia is simply superb. The bloom and five deeply serrated leaves are set in clear crystal. $2650.

212. ANTIQUE ST. LOUIS

Nine complex millefiori canes decorate the center of this panel weight. White spokes divide the red-and-white and blue-and-white jasper panels. $450.

213. ANTIQUE ST. LOUIS

Deeply serrated leaves surround a salmon-pink double clematis and red bud, dramatically displayed on a blue-and-white jasper ground. $1250.

214. ANTIQUE ST. LOUIS

In this classic nosegay weight, four typical St. Louis millefiori canes imitate tiny flowers set on five green leaves. The weight floats in clear crystal surrounded by a garland of complex canes. $785.

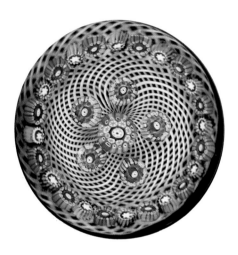

215. ANTIQUE ST. LOUIS

Complex millefiori canes in an unusual combination of colors rest on a well-formed latticinio cushion in this fine example of a patterned millefiori weight. $850.

216. ANTIQUE ST. LOUIS

This exquisite upright bouquet features many delicate blooms in various colors surrounded by eight serrated leaves. The bouquet is encircled by a salmon-colored torsade at the base of the stem. The weight is faceted overall. $3250.

217. ANTIQUE ST. LOUIS

An unusual blue-and-white turban swirl studded with eight complex millefiori canes forms the center of this red-and-blue jasper panel weight. $400.

218. ANTIQUE ST. LOUIS

Typical St. Louis overall faceting plays visual tricks making this two-flower bouquet, featuring a pansy and a small blue clematis, appear to be many different flowers. $1500.

219. ANTIQUE ST. LOUIS

Five delicate millefiori canes with arrow cane centers surround a larger central complex cane. The whole motif is set on a red-and-white jasper ground. $400.

220. ANTIQUE ST. LOUIS

This pretty upright bouquet with a white clematis and millefiori cane flowers is encircled by a beautiful blue and white torsade.
$2400.

221. ANTIQUE ST. LOUIS

A simple motif elegantly done, these two ripe red cherries on a stem with three green leaves look just right for picking. *$2850.*

222. ANTIQUE ST. LOUIS

This beautiful mushroom features a selection of St. Louis' finest canes set in a close concentric pattern. The mushroom tuft is encircled by a blue spiral torsade. *$2850.*

223. ANTIQUE ST. LOUIS

This is a superb example of a St. Louis pansy. Many flowers of this type still grow in the village gardens of St. Louis les-Bitches.

$1200.

224. ANTIQUE ST. LOUIS

A lacy blue spiral surrounds this upright bouquet of unusual configuration. Fancy faceting multiplies the design of the torsade.

$2800.

225. ANTIQUE ST. LOUIS

Beautiful in its simplicity, this St. Louis interpretation of the graceful fuchsia blossom and berry is set on a fine white latticinio cushion.

$3000.

GLOSSARY

Air Ring An elongated air inclusion encircling a weight near the base, usually above and below a torsade.

Arrow Cane A millefiori section made from rods containing a three-pronged arrow motif.

Base The bottom of a paperweight.

Basket An outer row of millefiori canes, pulled together underneath the motif to form a staved enclosure for the decorative elements; A latticinio ground pulled down in the center (as in St Louis and American fruit weights.)

Bouquet A floral design comprising more than one flower.

Cane The small piece of a molded or bundled glass rod that has been pulled out so that an intricate pattern appears in cross-section.

Carpet Ground An overall pattern of identical millefiori canes used as a backdrop for a pattern of other canes or decorative elements.

Chequer Weight A paperweight in which the millefiori canes are separated by short lengths of latticinio twists in a checkerboard fashion.

Cinquefoil A garland of canes having five loops.

Clear Ground Term used for a weight in which the motif rests on clear glass.

Close Concentric Millefiori A common spacing scheme in millefiori weights featuring tightly packed concentric circles of canes.

Close Millefiori General name for any spacing scheme in millefiori weights which features tightly packed random arrangement of canes.

Color Ground Term used when transparent or opaque colored glass has been used as the background for a paperweight motif.

Edelweiss Cane A white millefiori cane of star shape surrounding a core of bundled yellow rods—resembling the Swiss national flower.

Facet The flat or concave surface formed when the side or top (or both) of a paperweight is shaped with a flat or rounded grinding wheel.

Floret See CANE.

Garland General name for any spacing scheme in millefiori weights which features one or more chains of canes.

Hand Cooler An egg-shaped paperweight, once a common accessory for ladies.

Jasper Ground Paperweight backdrop formed by a mixture of two colors of finely ground glass.

Lace (Muslin or Upset Muslin) White or colored glass thread spiralled around a clear rod. Short lengths are used in a jumbled arrangement to form a background for the decorative elements.

Latticinio A swirl or spiral arrangement of many white or colored threads of glass used as a paperweight ground.

Magnum A paperweight with a diameter exceeding 3 inches.

Millefiori From the Italian phrase for "a thousand flowers." Used to describe the composite glass cross-section used in many paperweights.

Miniature A paperweight with a diameter of less than 2 inches.

Muslin see LACE.

Nosegay A motif consisting of a flat bouquet using millefiori canes as flowers.

Overlay Weight A paperweight that has been coated with one (single overlay), two (double overlay), or three (triple overlay) layers of glass and then had windows or facets cut in it to allow visual access to the inner motif. Flash overlays are coated with translucent glass before cutting.

Piedouche French term for footed weight.

Pinchbeck Weight Metallic disk made of a zinc-copper alloy and featuring a design in bas-relief. The disk is covered with a magnifying lens which is then fitted to a pewter or alabaster base.

Quatrefoil A four-lobed design used as a garland pattern; a faceting scheme.

Rod A cylindrical length of glass, most often containing a simple molded design of more than one color; the basic component of a millefiori cane.

Scrambled Millefiori A millefiori paperweight design in which whole and broken canes, and sometimes white or colored lace are jumbled together to fill the weight.

Signature Cane A millefiori cane bearing the name or initials of the weight's factory of origin or artist who created it.

Silhouette Cane A millefiori cane which in cross-section reveals the silhouette of an animal, flower, or human figure.

Star Cut A many-pointed star incised into the base of a weight for decoration.

Sulphide A three dimensional ceramic medallion or portrait plaque used as a decorative enclosure for a paperweight or other glass object.

Torsade An opaque glass thread loosely wound around a filigree core, usually found near the base of a mushroom weight.

Trefoil A garland with three loops.

Upright Bouquet A three-dimensional grouping of canes and stylized lampwork flowers set on a bed of leaves.

SULPHIDES
REFERENCE LISTS

REFERENCE LISTS OF CONTEMPORARY
BACCARAT SULPHIDES AND GRIDEL ANIMALS

BACCARAT

Subject	Regular	Overlay
Coronation	1492	195
Eisenhower	1389	178
Lincoln	1291	197
Washington	1182	200
Churchill	558	81
Jefferson	594	156
Queen Elizabeth		200
Robert E. Lee	913	137
Franklin	414	180
Lafayette	744	227
Luther	607	86
Pope Pius	2157	284
Sam Rayburn	512	93
J. F. Kennedy	3572	308
J. F. Kennedy (memorial)	314	
Pope John	775	343
T. Roosevelt	2359	381
Pierre Loval	160	100
A. Stevenson	2595	472
Will Rogers	2517	389
James Monroe	2500	400
Herbert Hoover	2500	400
Eleanor Roosevelt	2500	400
Andrew Jackson	2500	400
Woodrow Wilson	2400	400
Harry Truman	2400	400
Napoleon Bonaparte	2400	400
Napoleon Bonaparte (memorial)	100	
Thomas Paine	2000	400
Mt. Rushmore		1000
Patrick Henry	1500	400
Queen Elizabeth Jubilee	500	
Martin Luther King	500	

GRIDEL ANIMALS

Subject	Date Issued
1. Squirrel	1971-2
2. Rooster	1971
3. Elephant	1973
4. Horse	1973
5. Swan	1974
6. Pelican	1974
7. Hunter	1974
8. Pheasant	1975
9. Monkey (black)	1975
10. Deer (black)	1976
11. Monkey (white)	1976
12. Lovebirds	1977
13. Devil	1977
14. Stork	1977
15. Dog	1978
16. Goat	1978
17. Bird	1979
18. Butterfly	1979

The Rooster and Squirrel were issued in quantities of 1200; each subsequent edition is limited to not more than 350 pieces.

REFERENCE LISTS OF CONTEMPORARY
CRISTAL D'ALBRET AND ST. LOUIS SULPHIDES

CRISTAL D'ALBRET

Subject	Regular	Overlay
Columbus	1000	200
F. D. Roosevelt	2000	300
J. F. & Mrs. Kennedy	2000	
(experimental)		121
King of Sweden	1000	none
J. F. & Mrs. Kennedy	none	300
Leonardo da Vinci	1000	200
D. MacArthur	1500	300
Mark Twain	1000	225
Ernest Hemingway	1000	225
Paul Revere	800	200
Albert Schweitzer	1000	200
Prince Charles	1000	200
Moon Astronauts	1000	200
John J. Audubon	1000	225
Jenny Lind	410	170
John Paul Jones	430	170
Charles Lindbergh	400	170
Sitting Bull		
(Terracotta)	500	
(Tri-color)	500	
Mahatma Gandhi		
(Terracotta)	500	
(Tri-color)	500	
Martin Luther King		
(Tri-color)	325	
Ronald Reagan	500	300

ST. LOUIS

Queen Elizabeth
General Francois Ingold
Marquis de La Fayette
King Saint Louis
Robert Schuman
Iranian Monarchy
Autun Cathedral
General De Gaulle
    (as president)
Suita "Mon"
U.S. Eagle
General De Gaulle
    (in 1940)
Jimmy Carter
Amour
Pope John Paul II

PAPERWEIGHT • PRESS
SANTA CRUZ • CALIFORNIA